ISBN-13: 9798859034703
ISBN-10: 1477123456

Cover design by: Mariella Peters
Library of Congress Control Number: 2018675309
Printed in the United States of America

To my incredible support team,

*I dedicate this book to my loving children and my amazing
husband, who have been the driving force behind my journey
as an author. Your unwavering belief in me and your constant
encouragement have been the cornerstone of my success.*

*To my children, Calee, Haelyn, and Hayden, your boundless
curiosity, imagination, and belief in God inspire me every day.
You remind me of the power of storytelling and the joy that can
be found in every adventure. Thank you for sharing in my dreams
and for understanding when Mommy disappeared into the world
of words.*

*To my dearest husband, Tom, your unwavering support, patience,
and love have been my rock throughout this writing process.
You have believed in me even when I doubted myself, and your
words of encouragement have lifted me up during moments of
uncertainty. Thank you for standing by my side, cheering me on,
and sharing this remarkable journey together.*

*This book is a testament to our bond as a family and the
incredible strength we draw from one another. You have
sacrificed your time and made countless sacrifices to ensure that
I could pursue my passion for writing and entrepreneurship.
Your belief in me has given me the courage to chase my dreams
fearlessly, and I am forever grateful.*

*To my support team, my kids, and my amazing husband, thank
you for being the guiding light in my life. Your love, laughter, and
unwavering belief in me have made this book possible. May these
pages be a tribute to our shared adventures and a reminder of
the profound love that fills our home. Also, I want to thank you,
God, for the life you have blessed me with, for the talents and
gifts you have bestowed upon me, and for the opportunities that
have shaped me into the person I am today. Your divine grace has
carried me through the challenges and triumphs, reminding me
of your infinite love and boundless mercy.*

With all my love,

Mommy aka Mariella Peters

CONTENTS

Copyright

Dedication

Learning Money   1

Introduction   2

CHAPTER 1: Understanding Money   6

CHAPTER 2: The Birth of Cryptocurrency   17

CHAPTER 3: Who is Satoshi Nakamoto   22

CHAPTER 4: The Backbone of Cryptocurrency   28

CHAPTER 5: Cryptocurrency Ecosystem   34

CHAPTER 6: Altcoins - Diversification and Innovation   38

CHAPTER 7: Advantages and Challenges of Cryptocurrency   43

CHAPTER 8: Challenges and Concerns of Cryptocurrency   48

CHAPTER 9: Cryptocurrency - Education and Resources   53

CHAPTER 10: Websites and Online Platforms   56

CHAPTER 11: Crypto Skills - A Guide to Safety, Strategy, and Community Engagement   59

CHAPTER 12: Participating and Staying Updated in the Crypto Community   63

About The Author   71

Disclaimer   73

LEARNING MONEY

*Exploring the Origins
and Significance of
Cryptocurrency*

INTRODUCTION

This comprehensive book dives into the various aspects of money, cryptocurrencies, blockchain technology, and the evolving financial landscape. Explore topics such as the rise of digital payments, advantages and challenges of digital money, the genesis of Bitcoin, the power of blockchain technology, altcoins' innovation, the need for a new financial system, and the importance of ongoing learning in the crypto space.

Discover the key features of cryptocurrencies, including decentralization, transparency, and security. Delve into the historical evolution of money, from the barter system to fiat currencies, and understand why there is a desire for decentralized financial systems. Uncover the mystery surrounding Satoshi Nakamoto, the enigmatic creator of Bitcoin, and explore the core principles and goals outlined in the Bitcoin whitepaper.

Learn about blockchain technology, its role as the backbone of cryptocurrencies, and its ability to ensure security, immutability, and decentralization. Gain insights into the world of altcoins, such as Ethereum, Litecoin, and Ripple, and discover their unique features and use cases. Understand the advantages and challenges of cryptocurrencies, including global accessibility, transparency, volatility, regulatory considerations, and security risks.

Embark on a journey of education and skill development in the crypto space. Explore resources such as books, websites, and courses to expand your knowledge and understanding. Master wallet security, private key management, and safe trading strategies. Engage with the crypto community, stay updated with developments, and adapt to the ever-evolving landscape.

Embrace the potential of cryptocurrencies while remaining mindful of the risks and challenges. Stay informed, continue learning, and adapt to the dynamic world of digital finance. Discover the transformative power of cryptocurrencies and become an active participant in shaping the future of finance.

CHAPTER 1:

UNDERSTANDING

MONEY

Money serves as a medium of exchange, unit of account, and store of value. It has specific characteristics that differentiate it from other forms of wealth and assets.

Money can be defined as a universally accepted medium of exchange that facilitates the buying and selling of goods and services. It acts as a common denominator in transactions, eliminating the need for direct barter.

The primary purpose of money is to streamline economic activities. It serves as a unit of account, enabling the measurement and comparison of the value of goods and services. Additionally, money acts as a store of value, allowing individuals to accumulate wealth and transfer it across time and space.

Money performs three essential functions in an economy: it serves as a medium of exchange, a unit of account, and a store of value.

Money as a medium of exchange simplifies transactions by eliminating the need for a double coincidence of wants, which is required in barter systems. With money, individuals can acquire goods and services by exchanging it for the desired item.

Money acts as a standard unit of measurement for value, making it easier to compare the worth of different goods and services. By assigning a numerical value to items, money enables individuals to assess the relative prices and make informed economic decisions.

As a store of value, money allows individuals to save and accumulate wealth for future use. By holding money, individuals can defer consumption and preserve their purchasing power over time. However, the value of money can be affected by inflation and other economic factors.

Throughout history, various forms of money have emerged, reflecting the needs and preferences of different societies.

In early human societies, barter systems were prevalent. People exchanged goods directly, relying on a mutual coincidence of wants. However, barter systems had limitations, such as the lack of divisibility, indivisibility of certain goods, and the need for a double coincidence of wants.

To overcome the limitations of barter, societies

began using commodity money. Commodity money is a physical object with intrinsic value, such as shells, beads, or precious metals. It held value both as a medium of exchange and as a commodity itself.

With the rise of centralized authorities, fiat money emerged. Fiat money has value because the government declares it as legal tender. It is not backed by a physical commodity but relies on the trust and confidence of the people. Fiat currencies, such as the US dollar or the euro, dominate global economies today.

Money has played a vital role in human civilization, evolving from barter systems to sophisticated fiat currencies. As a medium of exchange, unit of account, and store of value, money has facilitated economic transactions and shaped societies. Understanding the functions and historical evolution of money allows us to appreciate its significance and adapt to the changing landscape of finance and commerce.

In the modern era, digital payments and electronic transactions have become increasingly prevalent, revolutionizing the way we conduct financial transactions. We'll delve into the advantages and challenges of digital money and introduces cryptocurrencies as a form of digital currency. By examining the transformative power of digital payments and understanding the unique features of cryptocurrencies, we can gain a comprehensive understanding of the evolving financial landscape.

Digital money offers numerous benefits that have contributed to its rise in popularity. Digital payments provide unparalleled convenience, allowing individuals to make transactions anytime and anywhere. The accessibility of digital money has enabled financial inclusion, reaching individuals who previously lacked access to traditional banking services.

Digital transactions are highly efficient, eliminating the need for physical cash and reducing administrative tasks associated with traditional payment methods. With instant fund transfers, digital money enables quick and seamless transactions.

Digital payments offer advanced security features such as encryption and authentication, ensuring the integrity and confidentiality of transactions. Compared to physical cash, digital money minimizes the risk of theft and fraud. Despite its advantages, digital money also presents several challenges that must be addressed.

The widespread use of digital transactions raises concerns about privacy and data security. Safeguarding personal information and protecting against unauthorized access or data breaches is a crucial challenge in the digital realm.

To fully embrace digital payments, a robust technological infrastructure and reliable internet connectivity are essential. However, the digital divide poses challenges, as not everyone has equal access to these resources, particularly in underserved areas.

The rise of digital money has attracted the attention of cybercriminals who exploit vulnerabilities in digital payment systems. Addressing cybersecurity risks and implementing robust measures to safeguard against cyber threats is crucial to ensure the security and trustworthiness of digital transactions.

Cryptocurrencies have emerged as a prominent form of digital currency, offering unique features and capabilities.

Cryptocurrencies are digital or virtual currencies that utilize cryptographic technology to secure transactions and control the creation of new units. They operate on decentralized networks, independent of central banks or government control.

Cryptocurrencies rely on blockchain technology, a decentralized and transparent ledger system, to record and verify transactions. The use of blockchain technology enhances security, eliminates the need for intermediaries, and fosters trust among participants.

The rise of digital payments has transformed the financial landscape, offering numerous advantages in terms of convenience, efficiency, and enhanced security. However, challenges related to privacy, infrastructure, and cybersecurity must be addressed to ensure widespread adoption and trust in digital money.

Additionally, the emergence of cryptocurrencies as a form of digital currency introduces new possibilities and challenges, with blockchain technology playing a pivotal role in reshaping financial transactions. By understanding the advantages, challenges, and potential of digital money and cryptocurrencies, we can navigate the evolving financial landscape and harness the benefits they offer.

CHAPTER 2:

THE BIRTH OF

CRYPTOCURRENCY

The traditional banking system has long served as the cornerstone of global finance, but in recent years, criticisms have emerged regarding its centralized control and lack of transparency. The need for a new financial system that addresses these concerns and embraces decentralization, transparency, and security.

By analyzing the criticisms of traditional banking and understanding the desire for a more inclusive and trustworthy system, we can shed light on the growing movement towards alternative financial models.

The traditional banking system has failed to provide equal access to financial services, leaving a significant portion of the population unbanked or underbanked. This lack of inclusivity perpetuates social and economic inequality.

Critics argue that traditional banking is excessively centralized, with a handful of large financial institutions exerting significant control over the global financial system. This concentration of power raises concerns about accountability, decision-making, and the potential for abuse.

The lack of transparency in traditional banking, including complex fee structures, hidden charges, and undisclosed risks, erodes trust and leaves consumers at a disadvantage. The opacity of the system contributes to financial instability and fosters a culture of secrecy.

Many individuals and organizations advocate for decentralized financial systems that distribute control and decision-making power. Decentralization promotes a more democratic and inclusive approach to finance, reducing the dependence on a few centralized authorities.

Transparency is a key element desired in a new financial system. The ability to track transactions, verify records, and have open access to information fosters trust among participants. Transparent financial systems promote accountability and enable individuals to make informed decisions.

The desire for a more secure financial system stems from concerns over data breaches, identity theft, and fraud. With decentralized technologies such as blockchain, which offer enhanced security and encryption, individuals seek a more robust and trustworthy framework for financial transactions.

The traditional banking system has faced criticism due to its centralized control, lack of transparency, and limited financial inclusion. These shortcomings have fueled the desire for a new financial system that embraces decentralization, transparency, and security.

As technology advances, alternative financial models are emerging, offering the potential for a more inclusive and trustworthy system. By addressing the criticisms and embracing the desire for change, we can pave the way for a new era of finance that prioritizes decentralization, transparency, and security.

CHAPTER 3: WHO IS SATOSHI NAKAMOTO

The emergence of Bitcoin, the world's first decentralized cryptocurrency, revolutionized the financial landscape and introduced a new era of digital currencies. At the heart of this groundbreaking development lies the enigmatic figure of Satoshi Nakamoto.

The background and mystery surrounding Satoshi

Nakamoto, explores the publication of the Bitcoin whitepaper in 2008, and examines the core principles and goals of Bitcoin as outlined by Nakamoto. By unraveling the story behind Bitcoin's genesis, we can gain a deeper understanding of its significance and the visionary ideas that have shaped the cryptocurrency movement.

The Background and Mystery of Satoshi Nakamoto is the pseudonymous individual or group responsible for the creation of Bitcoin. Despite the significant impact of Bitcoin on the financial world, Nakamoto's true identity remains unknown, adding an aura of mystery to the genesis of the cryptocurrency.

Shortly after the introduction of Bitcoin, Nakamoto vanished from public view, leaving the cryptocurrency community and the world at large speculating about the reasons behind the anonymity and subsequent disappearance. Various theories and claims have emerged, but Nakamoto's true identity and motives remain elusive.

In October 2008, Satoshi Nakamoto published a seminal document titled "Bitcoin: A Peer-to-Peer Electronic Cash System." This whitepaper laid the foundation for Bitcoin and outlined the fundamental principles and mechanisms behind the cryptocurrency.

The Bitcoin whitepaper introduced several groundbreaking concepts, including the decentralized blockchain technology, proof-of-work consensus mechanism, and the idea of a peer-to-peer electronic cash system. These innovations addressed long-standing challenges in digital currencies, such as double-spending and the need for trusted intermediaries.

Satoshi Nakamoto envisioned Bitcoin as a decentralized system, free from the control of central banks and governments. By relying on a distributed network of participants and the transparent nature of the blockchain, Bitcoin aims to eliminate the need for intermediaries and foster trust among users.

One of the core goals of Bitcoin is to provide financial inclusion to individuals who are unbanked or underserved by traditional financial institutions. Bitcoin's accessibility and borderless nature allow anyone with an internet connection to participate in the global economy.

Nakamoto emphasized the importance of privacy and security in financial transactions. Bitcoin transactions are pseudonymous, offering users a certain degree of privacy. The cryptographic security of the blockchain ensures the integrity and immutability of transaction records.

Satoshi Nakamoto's contribution to the world of finance through the creation of Bitcoin is nothing short of revolutionary. Despite the mystery surrounding Nakamoto's true identity, the publication of the Bitcoin whitepaper and the subsequent emergence of cryptocurrencies have transformed the way we perceive and engage with money.

Nakamoto's core principles of decentralization, financial inclusion, privacy, and security have resonated with individuals seeking a more transparent and equitable financial system. As the legacy of Satoshi Nakamoto continues to shape the cryptocurrency movement, Bitcoin stands as a testament to the power of innovation and the potential for transformative change in the realm of finance.

CHAPTER 4: THE BACKBONE OF CRYPTOCURRENCY

Blockchain technology has emerged as a revolutionary innovation that underpins the functioning of cryptocurrencies. The concept of blockchain, its role in ensuring security, immutability, and decentralization, and the significance of cryptocurrency mining and consensus mechanisms.

By understanding the fundamental principles of blockchain technology, we can appreciate its transformative potential in various industries beyond cryptocurrencies.

Blockchain is a decentralized and distributed digital ledger that records transactions across multiple computers or nodes. It operates on the principles of transparency, immutability, and consensus, enabling secure and trustworthy transactions.

A blockchain consists of blocks that store batches of transactions. Each block contains a cryptographic hash, timestamp, and a reference to the previous block, forming a chain. The distributed nature of blockchain ensures that all participants have access to the same information, creating a transparent and tamper-resistant system.

Blockchain employs cryptographic algorithms to secure data and transactions. Digital signatures, hash functions, and public-key cryptography ensure the authenticity, integrity, and confidentiality of information, making it difficult for malicious actors to alter or manipulate the blockchain.

Once a block is added to the blockchain, it becomes virtually impossible to modify or delete the recorded data. The consensus mechanism and cryptographic hash functions ensure the immutability of previous blocks, providing a transparent and auditable transaction history.

Blockchain eliminates the need for a central authority or intermediary, empowering participants to transact directly with each other. Consensus mechanisms, such as proof-of-work (PoW) or proof-of-stake (PoS), enable nodes to agree on the validity of transactions, ensuring consensus and preventing fraudulent activities.

Cryptocurrency mining is the process of validating and adding transactions to the blockchain. Miners use computational power to solve complex mathematical problems, contributing to the security and integrity of the blockchain. In return for their efforts, miners are rewarded with newly minted cryptocurrency coins.

Proof-of-Work (PoW) is the most commonly used consensus mechanism in blockchain networks, as seen in Bitcoin. Miners compete to solve complex puzzles, and the first one to find the solution validates the block. This mechanism ensures security and prevents double-spending attacks.

Other consensus mechanisms, such as proof-of-stake (PoS), delegated proof-of-stake (DPoS), and Byzantine fault tolerance (BFT), offer alternative approaches to achieving consensus. These mechanisms prioritize factors such as coin ownership, reputation, or voting power in determining block validation.

Blockchain technology serves as the foundational

backbone of cryptocurrencies, providing security, immutability, and decentralization to digital transactions. By understanding the concept of blockchain, its inherent security measures, and the role of consensus mechanisms, we can grasp the transformative potential of this technology beyond the realm of cryptocurrencies.

As blockchain continues to evolve and find applications in various industries, it holds the promise of revolutionizing systems, fostering trust, and empowering individuals in an increasingly digital world.

CHAPTER 5:

CRYPTOCURRENCY

ECOSYSTEM

Bitcoin, the first and most well-known cryptocurrency, has brought about a paradigm shift in the world of finance. It aimed to create a decentralized digital currency that operates outside the control of central banks and governments. Bitcoin operates on a blockchain, a distributed ledger that records and verifies transactions.

The blockchain ensures transparency, security, and immutability by storing transaction data across a network of computers or nodes as briefly discussed in chapter 2. One of Bitcoin's defining characteristics is its limited supply. Only 21 million bitcoins will ever exist, which adds to its scarcity and potential value. This finite supply distinguishes Bitcoin from traditional fiat currencies and has contributed to its appeal as a store of value.

Bitcoin transactions are pseudonymous, meaning that they do not directly reveal the identity of the individuals involved. While transactions are recorded on the public blockchain, the identities behind the addresses are not readily discernible, providing a certain level of privacy.

Bitcoin's decentralized nature empowers individuals to have control over their finances. It eliminates the need for intermediaries like banks, enabling users to transact directly with one another. This financial sovereignty offers individuals greater autonomy and removes barriers to financial inclusion.

Bitcoin has challenged traditional financial systems by providing an alternative means of transferring value globally. Its borderless nature allows for faster and more cost-effective cross-border transactions compared to traditional banking systems, which often involve lengthy processes and high fees.

Bitcoin's price volatility has attracted significant attention from investors and speculators. Its potential for substantial gains, as well as risks, has sparked a vibrant market for trading and investment. Bitcoin's price movements have drawn both proponents and critics, contributing to ongoing debates about its long-term viability.

Bitcoin's impact extends beyond its technological innovations, sparking a global movement towards embracing cryptocurrencies and blockchain technology. As the cryptocurrency ecosystem continues to evolve, understanding Bitcoin's fundamentals and its role as a catalyst for change is crucial in navigating the future of digital finance.

CHAPTER 6: ALTCOINS - DIVERSIFICATION AND INNOVATION

While Bitcoin paved the way for cryptocurrencies, a diverse ecosystem of alternative cryptocurrencies, commonly known as altcoins, has emerged. These altcoins offer unique features and use cases, providing users with a range of options beyond Bitcoin. The concept of altcoins, highlights prominent examples such as Ethereum, Litecoin, and Ripple, and examines their distinct characteristics and innovative contributions to the cryptocurrency landscape.

Altcoins refer to any cryptocurrency other than Bitcoin. They were created to address perceived limitations of Bitcoin and to offer additional functionalities, use cases, and innovations. Altcoins provide diversification within the cryptocurrency market, allowing investors and users to explore different blockchain platforms, applications, and technologies beyond the scope of Bitcoin.

Ethereum is a decentralized platform that enables the development of smart contracts and decentralized applications (DApps). Its native cryptocurrency, Ether (ETH), fuels the Ethereum network and serves as a utility token for executing smart contracts.

Litecoin was created as a "lite" version of Bitcoin, aiming to improve transaction speed and efficiency. It employs a different hashing algorithm, scrypt, and offers faster block generation times, making it more suitable for everyday transactions.

Ripple is both a digital payment protocol and a cryptocurrency (XRP). It facilitates fast, low-cost international money transfers and aims to bridge the gap between traditional financial systems and blockchain technology.

Altcoins like Ethereum have introduced the

concept of smart contracts, enabling self-executing agreements with predefined conditions. These contracts have applications across various industries, including finance, supply chain management, and decentralized governance.

Some altcoins, such as Monero and Zcash, emphasize privacy and anonymity features. They utilize advanced cryptographic techniques to obfuscate transaction details and provide enhanced privacy options for users.

Certain altcoins focus on specific use cases or industries. For instance, IOTA aims to facilitate transactions and data transfer within the Internet of Things (IoT) ecosystem, while Chainlink aims to provide decentralized oracle services, enabling smart contracts to interact with real-world data.

Altcoins have brought diversification and innovation to the cryptocurrency ecosystem, offering users a wider range of options beyond Bitcoin. Examples such as Ethereum, Litecoin, and Ripple showcase unique features and use cases, expanding the potential applications of blockchain technology.

As the altcoin market continues to evolve, it is crucial to understand the distinct characteristics and contributions of different altcoins. Embracing this diversity promotes innovation, drives adoption, and enhances the overall development of the cryptocurrency landscape.

CHAPTER 7:

ADVANTAGES AND CHALLENGES OF CRYPTOCURRENCY

Cryptocurrency has emerged as a disruptive force in the financial landscape, offering a range of advantages and presenting unique challenges. We'll explore the advantages of cryptocurrency, including decentralization, global accessibility, and transaction transparency. It also examines the challenges associated with this emerging technology, such as regulatory concerns and scalability issues.

Cryptocurrencies operate on decentralized blockchain networks, eliminating the need for intermediaries such as banks or payment processors. This decentralization fosters peer-to-peer transactions, reducing costs, and enhancing security.

Cryptocurrency transcends geographical boundaries, allowing individuals with internet access to participate in the digital economy.

It enables financial inclusion for the unbanked and underbanked populations worldwide, providing them with opportunities for secure and affordable financial services.

Transactions recorded on the blockchain are transparent and publicly accessible. This transparency enhances accountability and reduces the risk of fraud. Additionally, the immutability of blockchain transactions ensures that once recorded, they cannot be altered, adding a layer of security and trust to the system.

Cryptocurrencies operate in a regulatory grey area in many jurisdictions. Governments and regulatory bodies face challenges in establishing frameworks to govern these digital assets effectively. Concerns around money laundering, tax evasion, and consumer protection require careful consideration to strike a balance between innovation and regulation.

As the popularity of cryptocurrencies grows, scalability becomes a significant challenge. Blockchains, like Bitcoin's, can experience congestion and slower transaction speeds during periods of high demand. Achieving scalability without compromising decentralization and security is a key technical hurdle that the cryptocurrency community continues to address.

Cryptocurrencies are known for their price volatility. Rapid price fluctuations can pose risks for investors and hinder wider adoption for everyday transactions. Mitigating this volatility through increased stability mechanisms and improved market liquidity is essential for building trust and confidence in the long-term viability of cryptocurrencies.

Cryptocurrency offers numerous advantages, including decentralization, global accessibility, and transaction transparency, which have the potential to reshape the financial landscape. However, challenges such as regulatory concerns, scalability, and price volatility need to be addressed for the widespread adoption and acceptance of cryptocurrencies. By navigating these challenges and leveraging the benefits of this emerging technology, the path to a more inclusive, transparent, and efficient financial system becomes clearer.

CHAPTER 8: CHALLENGES AND CONCERNS OF CRYPTOCURRENCY

Cryptocurrency has revolutionized the financial landscape, offering exciting opportunities and innovative solutions. However, it also presents unique challenges and concerns that must be addressed for its widespread adoption and acceptance. The challenges and concerns associated with cryptocurrency, including volatility and price fluctuations, regulatory and legal considerations, and security risks.

Cryptocurrencies are known for their high volatility, characterized by rapid and significant price fluctuations. This volatility poses challenges for investors and users alike. Sudden price swings can result in substantial gains or losses, creating uncertainty and hindering the use of cryptocurrencies as a stable medium of exchange. Addressing volatility requires increased market liquidity, improved stability mechanisms, and the development of hedging tools to manage risks effectively.

The decentralized nature of cryptocurrencies challenges existing regulatory frameworks and raises legal concerns. Governments and regulatory bodies around the world grapple with defining the regulatory status of cryptocurrencies and establishing appropriate guidelines. Key considerations include anti-money laundering (AML) and know-your-customer (KYC) regulations, taxation policies, investor protection, and consumer rights. Striking a balance between fostering innovation and protecting the interests of stakeholders remains a complex task.

Cryptocurrency transactions occur on public blockchains, which offer transparency and immutability. However, they also introduce security risks and the potential for fraud. Cyberattacks, including hacking, phishing, and ransomware attacks, pose significant threats to individuals, exchanges, and wallet providers.

Moreover, the pseudonymous nature of cryptocurrency transactions can facilitate illicit activities such as money laundering and terrorist financing. Strengthening security measures, enhancing user education, and promoting industry best practices are crucial to mitigating these risks.

Cryptocurrency has the potential to revolutionize finance, but it is not without challenges and concerns. Volatility and price fluctuations hinder its stability as a medium of exchange, necessitating efforts to enhance market liquidity and stability mechanisms. Regulatory and legal considerations require thoughtful analysis to strike a balance between innovation and compliance.

Security risks and fraud must be addressed through robust security measures and increased awareness. By addressing these challenges and concerns, the cryptocurrency ecosystem can evolve into a more secure, regulated, and trusted financial system, unlocking the full potential of this transformative technology.

CHAPTER 9:

CRYPTOCURRENCY

- EDUCATION AND

RESOURCES

Cryptocurrency is a rapidly evolving field that has the potential to reshape the future of finance. As the interest in cryptocurrencies grows, it becomes increasingly important for individuals to educate themselves about this emerging technology. The importance of cryptocurrency education and provides recommendations for valuable resources that can facilitate the learning process.

Cryptocurrency is a complex subject that requires a foundational understanding of blockchain technology, cryptography, and decentralized systems. Educating oneself about these concepts helps individuals navigate the intricacies of cryptocurrencies and make informed decisions.

By learning about cryptocurrencies, individuals gain the knowledge and skills necessary to participate in the digital economy. This empowers them to take control of their financial future, diversify their investments, and explore new avenues for wealth creation.

There are several insightful books available that cater to different levels of knowledge and interests. Some recommended titles include "Mastering Bitcoin" by Andreas Antonopoulos, "Cryptocurrency: How Bitcoin and Digital Money are Challenging the Global Economic Order" by Paul Vigna and Michael J. Casey, and "The Age of Cryptocurrency" by Paul Vigna and Michael J. Casey.

CHAPTER 10:

WEBSITES AND

ONLINE PLATFORMS

Numerous websites and online platforms offer comprehensive resources on cryptocurrency. Websites like CoinDesk, CoinMarketCap, and Cointelegraph provide up-to-date news, analysis, and educational articles. Online learning platforms such as Udemy, Coursera, and

Khan Academy offer courses specifically designed to introduce learners to cryptocurrencies.

Engaging with cryptocurrency communities can be an invaluable source of learning. Platforms like Reddit, BitcoinTalk, and Telegram host active communities where users can ask questions, participate in discussions, and gain insights from experienced enthusiasts.

Podcasts such as "Unchained" and "The Bitcoin Podcast Network" feature interviews with industry experts and provide in-depth discussions on various cryptocurrency topics. YouTube channels like Andreas Antonopoulos and Ivan on Tech offer educational videos covering a wide range of cryptocurrency subjects.

In the fast-paced world of cryptocurrencies, education is crucial for individuals seeking to understand and navigate this emerging field successfully. By taking the initiative to learn about cryptocurrencies, individuals empower themselves with the knowledge necessary to make informed decisions and participate in the digital economy.

Through books, websites, online platforms, community forums, podcasts, and YouTube channels, there is a wealth of resources available to support the learning journey. By leveraging these educational resources, individuals can expand their understanding of cryptocurrencies and seize the opportunities presented by this transformative technology.

CHAPTER 11: CRYPTO SKILLS - A GUIDE TO SAFETY, STRATEGY, AND COMMUNITY ENGAGEMENT

As the world of cryptocurrencies continues to grow, developing the necessary skills becomes crucial for individuals seeking to navigate this evolving landscape successfully. The importance of developing crypto skills and provides insights into three key areas: wallet security and private key management, safe trading and investment strategies, and active participation in the crypto community.

The security of cryptocurrency wallets is paramount to protect digital assets. Understanding the different types of wallets, such as hardware wallets, software wallets, and paper wallets, helps individuals choose the most secure option that suits their needs.

Private keys are critical components for accessing and controlling cryptocurrencies. Learning best practices for generating strong private keys, storing them securely, and implementing multi-factor authentication ensures the safety of digital assets and minimizes the risk of unauthorized access.

Cryptocurrency markets can be volatile, and understanding risk management principles is essential. Concepts such as setting stop-loss orders, diversifying investments, and determining risk tolerance enable individuals to make informed decisions and protect their capital.

Developing basic knowledge of technical analysis tools, such as chart patterns, trendlines, and indicators, helps individuals analyze market trends and identify potential buying or selling opportunities. This skill enhances decision-making and improves the timing of trades.

Understanding fundamental analysis allows individuals to evaluate the long-term potential of cryptocurrencies. Learning about project fundamentals, team backgrounds, partnerships, and market adoption provides insights into the intrinsic value of different cryptocurrencies.

CHAPTER 12:

PARTICIPATING AND STAYING UPDATED IN THE CRYPTO COMMUNITY

Active participation in the crypto community opens avenues for learning, collaboration, and networking. Joining online forums, attending meetups, and engaging in discussions on social media platforms enable individuals to gain insights, share knowledge, and learn from experienced members.

Cryptocurrencies and blockchain technology are rapidly evolving fields. Staying informed about market trends, regulatory developments, and technological advancements is vital. Following reputable news sources, subscribing to industry newsletters, and attending conferences or webinars help individuals stay up to date.

Developing crypto skills is an ongoing journey that empowers individuals to navigate the dynamic world of cryptocurrencies with confidence. By understanding wallet security and private key management, individuals can safeguard their digital assets effectively. Implementing safe trading and investment strategies enables individuals to make informed decisions and manage risks.

Active participation in the crypto community fosters learning, collaboration, and networking opportunities. By staying updated with developments, individuals ensure they are well-informed about market trends and regulatory changes. By developing these essential skills, individuals are better equipped to seize opportunities, mitigate risks, and thrive in the exciting and transformative realm of cryptocurrencies.

Now that we have explored various aspects of cryptocurrencies, including their rise, advantages, challenges, and the need for a new financial system.

As well as we delved into the origins of Bitcoin, the fundamentals of blockchain technology, the diverse world of altcoins, and the advantages and concerns associated with cryptocurrencies. We have also discussed the importance of education, developed crypto skills, and stayed updated in this ever-evolving landscape.

One recurring theme is the importance of ongoing

learning and adaptation in the cryptocurrency space. Cryptocurrencies represent a paradigm shift in the way we think about money, finance, and technology.

To navigate this dynamic landscape successfully, individuals must embrace a mindset of continuous learning. Keeping up with the latest trends, understanding new developments, and honing necessary skills are essential for making informed decisions and maximizing the potential of cryptocurrencies.

While cryptocurrencies offer numerous advantages such as decentralization, global accessibility, and transparency, it is crucial to remain mindful of the risks and challenges they present. Volatility, regulatory considerations, security risks, and fraud are among the concerns that need to be addressed.

By understanding these risks and adopting best practices in areas like wallet security, trading strategies, and community engagement, individuals can navigate the cryptocurrency space more effectively and protect themselves from potential pitfalls.

To put it briefly, the world of cryptocurrencies presents a transformative opportunity for individuals seeking financial empowerment and technological innovation. By embracing ongoing learning, staying adaptable, and developing the necessary skills, we can harness the potential of cryptocurrencies to reshape our financial systems.

However, it is vital to approach this space with caution and awareness, understanding the risks and challenges involved. With a balanced perspective, informed decision-making, and a commitment to responsible engagement, we can embrace the potential of cryptocurrencies while mitigating risks and contributing to the continued growth and development of this exciting ecosystem. Until next time crypto explorers!

ABOUT THE AUTHOR

Mariella Peters

Mariella Peters is a passionate author and seasoned professional with a diverse range of skills and experiences. From a young age, she discovered her love for writing and storytelling, and her dedication to the craft has driven her to become the author of this informative book, "Learning Money: Exploring the Origins and Significance of Cryptocurrency"

With a lifelong passion for writing, Mariella Peters has honed her storytelling abilities over the years, allowing her skills to come alive on the pages of her books. Her commitment to her craft is evident in the material she creates.

Beyond her writing pursuits, Mariella Peters is also a successful financial consultant that specialize in crypto investing. As a motivational speaker and leadership development consultant. Armed with a degree from Albany University's business school, she was recruited by one of the top accounting firms in the world. Her expertise and passion for financial consulting led her to now deliver informational presentations/speeches that helps companies succeed and thrive.

When the onset of the Covid pandemic, Mariella Peters made the decision to prioritize her family and chose to stay home to care for her children. During this transformative period, she recognized the need for change and embarked on a journey of personal growth and entrepreneurship.

Today, Mariella Peters is excited to explore her diverse skill set and pursue various avenues of entrepreneurship, with writing being a central focus. Through her writing, she aims to captivate readers and transport them into imaginative and informational worlds filled with intrigue, emotion, and unforgettable learning experiences.

We invite you to delve into "Learning Money: Exploring the Origins and Significance of Cryptocurrency" and embark on a educational journey crafted by the talented and passionate author, Mariella Peters. Stay tuned for more of her engaging works as she continues to share her storytelling and educational teaching gifts with the world.

Thank you for your support, and happy reading!

DISCLAIMER

The information provided is for educational purposes only and should not be construed as financial or investment advice. It is essential to consult with a qualified financial professional or advisor before making any investment decisions. Remember, investing involves risks, and there is no guarantee of returns.